THE
BIG
TIME

LADY GAGA

AARON FRISCH

CREATIVE EDUCATION

LADY GAGA

TABLE OF CONTENTS

MEET LADY GAGA

Dance music thumps through big speakers. Lights flash. The crowd jumps around. Then Lady Gaga walks onto the stage wearing a mask. When she starts to sing, she turns the concert into a party!

Lady Gaga (whose real name is Stefani Germanotta) is a pop star who writes and sings mostly dance music. She is known for her fast songs. She is known for her strange outfits, too!

In 2010, Lady Gaga wore a dress made out of meat (right)

LADY GAGA'S CHILDHOOD

Stefani was born March 28, 1986, in New York, New York. She began playing piano at the age of four. When Stefani was 11, she started to go to a Catholic school for girls.

Lady Gaga still gives many performances in New York City

NEW YORK, NEW YORK

GETTING INTO MUSIC

When Stefani was in high school, she acted in school plays and sang in a band. After high school, Stefani studied music and theater at a New York college. But she soon left to start her music career.

··

Lady Gaga sometimes acts by dressing up as a man

Stefani formed a new band called the Stefani Germanotta Band. Her band played music in bars and **nightclubs**. In 2006, Stefani began calling herself Lady Gaga and performing by herself.

Flashy costumes and even motorcycles help make Lady Gaga's shows exciting

THE BIG TIME

I n 2008, Lady Gaga moved to Los Angeles, California. She released her first album, called *The Fame*. It had songs like "Just Dance" on it, and it was a hit. People bought more than 12 million copies of it!

Los Angeles is famous for its music

LOS ANGELES, CALIFORNIA

By 2009, Lada Gaga was a huge star. She became famous for the way she sang and danced in concerts and music videos. Her music won many honors, including five **_Grammy Awards_**.

....

Lady Gaga has won Grammy Awards for the best dance song and dance album

OFF THE STAGE

Besides music, Lady Gaga is very interested in art and *fashion*. Her hair is dark, but she usually dyes it to be blonde. Lady Gaga makes a lot of money but gives a lot to *charities*, too.

Lady Gaga likes to change her hairstyle and wear wild new outfits

WHAT IS NEXT?

In 2011, Lady Gaga released her third album, called *Born This Way*. It was another hit. In 2012, she traveled around the world doing concerts. She plans to keep people dancing for a long time!

....

Backup dancers usually perform with Lady Gaga

WHAT LADY GAGA SAYS ABOUT ...

BEING YOURSELF

"You have to be unique, and different, and shine in your own way."

FAME

"I've always been famous. It's just no one knew it yet."

HER FAMILY

"I am a real family girl. When it comes to love and loyalty, I am very old-fashioned."

GLOSSARY

charities groups that work to help other people

fashion a certain style or way of dressing

Grammy Awards the most famous music awards in the United States

nightclubs places where people go at night to hear music and dance

READ MORE

Aloian, Molly. *Lady Gaga*. New York: Crabtree, 2012.

Tieck, Sarah. *Lady Gaga: Singing Sensation*. Minneapolis: Abdo, 2011.

WEB SITES

Lady Gaga Biography
http://www.people.com/people/lady_gaga/
This site has information about Lady Gaga's life and many pictures, too.

Lady Gaga Coloring Pages
http://www.hellokids.com/r_1778/coloring-page/famous-people-coloring-pages/lady-gaga-coloring-pages
This site has pictures of Lady Gaga you can print out and color.

INDEX

PUBLISHED BY Creative Education
P.O. Box 227, Mankato, Minnesota 56002
Creative Education is an imprint of The Creative Company
www.thecreativecompany.us

DESIGN AND PRODUCTION BY Christine Vanderbeek
ART DIRECTION BY Rita Marshall
PRINTED IN the United States of America

PHOTOGRAPHS BY Alamy (ZUMA Wire Service), Getty Images (Jemal Countess, Kevork Djansezian, Jeff Kravitz/FilmMagic, Valerie Macon/AFP, Christopher Polk/Clear Channel, Andy Sheppard/Redferns, Soul Brother/FilmMagic), iStockphoto (GYI NSEA, Pingebat, Cole Vineyard), Shutterstock (Featureflash, s_bukley, vipflash)

LIBRARY OF CONGRESS CATALOGING-IN-PUBLICATION DATA
Frisch, Aaron.
Lady Gaga / Aaron Frisch.
p. cm. — (The big time)
Includes bibliographical references and index.
Summary: An elementary introduction to the life, work, and popularity of Lady Gaga, an American pop singer known for her eccentric and often controversial style and such songs as "Just Dance."

ISBN 978-1-60818-332-6
1. Lady Gaga—Juvenile literature. 2. Singers—United States—Biography—Juvenile literature. I. Title.
ML3930.L13F75 2013
782.42164092—dc23 [B] 2012013471

First edition
9 8 7 6 5 4 3 2 1